A Special Thank You!

As a special thank you for your book purchase, please log onto the following link below to download your free colouring book to print and enjoy!

Link:

www.amazinglycoolbooks.com/specialthankyou

Copyright © 2020 Natalie Murray

My Oh My! I Have Gorgeous Eyes
www.amazinglycoolbooks.com

The moral right of the author has been asserted.

All rights reserved. No part of this publication may be reproduced, stored in a retrieval system, or transmitted, in any form or by any means, electronic, mechanical, photocopying, recording, or otherwise, without prior written permission from the publisher.

Illustration by Sarah-Leigh Wills.
www.happydesigner.co.uk

DMJ Publising
www.dmjpublishing.co.uk

My Oh My!
I have gorgeous eyes

Written by
Natalie Murray

Illustrations by
Happydesigner

Look at my eyes.
My eyes are big.
My eyes are round.
My eyes are a beautiful shade of brown.

My eyes are slanted and very unique.
My eyes are great!
When something is hidden,
I can take a peek.

My eyes are a fabulous blue!
I love them so much.
I'm glad I have two!

My eyes are grey they are wonderful.
I am glad they are mine.
I wish I could keep my eyes
open all the time.

I am so happy my eyes are green.
I think they are the coolest eyes
I have ever seen.

My eyes need a little help
so I have some trendy glasses.
I wear them in school in all of my classes.

My eyes don't work
So, I can't see but I have a special friend
to help me.

He uses his eyes to do what I can't.
He can fetch and carry my toys, he plays
with me and the other girls and boys.

We are so happy
That we have our eyes.
They are so special
No matter what colour, shape or size

Other books in the series:

Have you got all 4?

www. amazinglycoolbooks.com

www.ingramcontent.com/pod-product-compliance
Lightning Source LLC
Chambersburg PA
CBHW081400080526
44588CB00016B/2560